A CHEER FOR MR. LEARY

by Bettina Hanson
illustrated by Albert Molnar

Harcourt

Orlando   Boston   Dallas   Chicago   San Diego

My name is Jane. I live on Greer Street near the bus stop. Mom and I take the bus a lot. We are waiting for the bus now.

I can hear the bus before I see
it. I know it is near my stop. When
the bus stops, Mom and I get on.

We say hello to Mr. Leary. He
has been our bus driver for years.
Mr. Leary has a white beard. It is
so thick that it hides his ears!

Mom and I sit near Mr. Leary.
I like to watch him drive. He steers
the bus by turning the big steering
wheel. He shifts the gears, too.

Mr. Leary stops at each bus stop.
People get off, and people get on.
Mr. Leary checks the rear of the
bus. Then he leaves the stop.

It is clear that Mr. Leary likes
his job. He always smiles from ear
to ear.

It is clear that the bus riders
like Mr. Leary, too. They always
say hello before they move to
the rear.

We are near the bus stop I like
the best. It is on Deer Road.
I always look for real, live deer,
but I never see any.

"Why is this road named Deer
Road?" I ask Mom. "Maybe deer
used to live nearby," Mom
tells me.